THE PERFECT SETTING COOKBOOK

PERI WOLFMAN & CHARLES GOLD

THE PERFECT SETTING COOKBOOK

HARRY N. ABRAMS, INC., PUBLISHERS

EDITOR • RUTH A. PELTASON
DESIGNER • ANNA R. MILLER

Grateful acknowledgment is made to the following publishers for
permission to reprint recipes: *The Soho Charcuterie Cookbook,* William
Morrow and Company, Inc., 1983; *The Silver Palate Cookbook,*
Workman Publishing Company, Inc., 1982; *Cosmopolitan* Magazine,
© 1983 The Hearst Corporation, for the following recipes:
*Cranberry/Maple Apples, Zesty Bosc Pears, Seckel Pears Almondine,
Oranges in Port Wine.*

The photographs on pages 82 and 86 are reprinted from *Cosmopolitan*
Magazine, © 1983 The Hearst Corporation.
The photograph on page 107 is reprinted from *House & Garden.*
Copyright 1980 by The Condé Nast Publications Inc.
The authors wish to thank the following photographers for permission
to reproduce their works:
Corrine Colen, Ken Druse, Brigitte Lacombe, Elyse Lewin, Russell
MacMasters, Chris Mead.

Library of Congress Catalog Card Number: 95–75708
ISBN 0–8109–3737–9

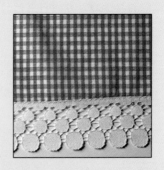

CONTENTS

MENU

+ Welcome +
all our friends
who come to dine
not merely to eat!

P & C

RECIPES

IT SEEMS AS IF EVERYONE WAS A GOURMET COOK in the 1970s. Nothing was too much work or took too long to prepare. Simply put, we had become a sophisticated food society. But when friends arrived for dinner, often we were too exhausted to enjoy their company. Fortunately for food and friendship this trend in cooking has changed direction, and we are no longer working hard to create elaborate meals. Today we enjoy foods that are light and simply prepared. Most importantly, we are cooking with seasonal and regional foods which have their own naturally good taste.

On the following pages are some of our favorite recipes and those of our friends. They all have three ingredients in common: They aren't complicated, they don't take a great deal of time to prepare, and they are tasty. Here, then, is to good food and good company.

BREAKFAST & BRUNCH

FRUIT BUTTERS

CANDIED BACON

BREAKFAST HASH BROWNS

MORNING GLORY MUFFINS

POPOVER PANCAKE

AEBLESKIVER
(DANISH RAISED PANCAKES)

BUCKWHEAT CRÊPES WITH CAVIAR

Fruit Butters

Fruit-flavored butters are tasty with warm breakfast muffins and breads, and surprisingly good on biscuits served with lunch.

Strawberry Butter

1 stick (8 tablespoons) sweet butter
4 ripe strawberries, cored and sliced
2 teaspoons dark brown sugar
Pinch of salt

Place all ingredients in bowl of food processor and blend for 1 minute. Spoon into a small ramekin, mounding the top.

ORANGE BUTTER

1 stick (8 tablespoons) sweet butter
2 teaspoons grated orange rind
2 teaspoons orange juice
1 teaspoon dark brown sugar
Pinch of salt

Follow directions for Strawberry Butter.

CANDIED BACON

A REAL BREAKFAST TREAT FOR ANYONE WHO WAKES UP
with a sweet tooth.

¼ pound dark brown sugar
1 pound bacon, at room temperature

Heat oven to 350°. Spread the brown sugar on wax paper. Press
each strip of bacon into sugar, coating both sides. Arrange flat
on 11-by-13-inch jelly-roll pan. Cook for about 30 minutes.
Remove from oven. Using 2 forks (it will be scalding hot—do
not touch) roll each strip of bacon, jelly-roll style. Place on a
china plate to cool before eating.

DEPENDING ON YOUR GROUP, ENOUGH FOR 4-6 PEOPLE

Breakfast Hash Browns

These hash browns are tangy when made with leftover Potatoes Vinaigrette.

3 tablespoons butter
1 onion, sliced
Potatoes Vinaigrette (page 54)

In large skillet, melt butter. When hot, add onions and potatoes. Sauté until golden brown.

Serve with eggs (any style) and sausage, ham, or bacon.

Morning Glory Muffins

THE COMBINATION OF FRUIT AND NUTS MAKES THESE muffins from Nantucket's Morning Glory Café a wonderful breakfast treat.

2 ½ cups sugar

4 cups flour

4 teaspoons cinnamon

4 teaspoons baking soda

1 teaspoon salt

1 cup raisins, plumped in brandy and drained

1 cup coconut, shredded

4 cups shredded carrots

2 apples, shredded

1 cup pecans

6 eggs

2 cups vegetable oil

1 teaspoon vanilla extract

Heat oven to 375°. Sift dry ingredients into a large bowl. Lightly dust the raisins with flour. Add the coconut, carrots, fruit, and nuts, and stir well. Add the eggs, oil, and vanilla, stirring only until combined.

Spoon batter into cupcake tins and bake for 20 minutes. Muffins should "ripen" for 24 hours for maximum blending of flavors.

MAKES 16–20 MUFFINS

Popover Pancake

Τ HIS PANCAKE IS SPECTACULAR TO SERVE, DELICIOUS TO EAT, and easy to prepare.

½ cup flour
½ cup milk
2 eggs, lightly beaten
4 grinds or 2 shakes of nutmeg
4 tablespoons butter
2 tablespoons confectioners' sugar
Juice of ½ lemon
Fresh fruit or jam (optional)

Heat oven to 425°. In a mixing bowl combine the first 4 ingredients and beat well with rotary beater. Melt butter in a cast iron enamel-coated 8-inch omelette pan with heatproof handle (this is the only pan in which the pancake sides rise and puff up). When the butter is very hot (sizzling) pour in batter. Cook on top of the stove over medium-low heat for a few minutes to set. Do not stir. Bake in oven for 20 minutes until puffy and golden. Sprinkle with sugar and return to oven for a few more minutes. Sprinkle with lemon juice and serve at once, with fresh fruit or jam, if desired.

SERVES 1 VERY HUNGRY PERSON FOR BRUNCH

SERVES 4 AS DESSERT

Aebleskiver (Danish Raised Pancakes)

An aebleskiver pan is a cast-iron "frying pan" with indentations the size and shape of a small orange. It is a must for this recipe.

4 cups flour
1 tablespoon sugar
1 teaspoon salt
1 teaspoon ground cardamom
3 tablespoons double-acting baking powder
3 cups milk
4 eggs, separated
⅓ cup beer
Juice of ½ lemon
Grated rind of 1 lemon
Shortening
Confectioners' sugar

Combine the first 5 ingredients in a large bowl. Mix together the milk and egg yolks; beat into the dry ingredients. Add the beer, lemon juice, and rind. Beat the egg whites until stiff, but not dry, and fold into the batter.

Heat the aebleskiver pan and put 1 teaspoon of shortening into each well. Test heat by dropping in a little batter; if it forms a shape immediately the shortening is ready. However, the pan

should not be so hot that the pancakes brown too quickly and remain uncooked in the middle. Put only about 1 rounded tablespoon of batter in each well. When batter becomes golden, turn with a fork and cook on the other side, about 5 to 6 minutes. Drain on a paper towel. Refill well each time with more shortening. Sprinkle with confectioners' sugar.

MAKES ABOUT 4 DOZEN PANCAKES

Buckwheat Crêpes with Caviar

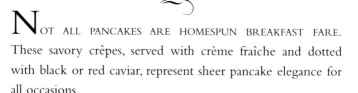

Not all pancakes are homespun breakfast fare. These savory crêpes, served with crème fraîche and dotted with black or red caviar, represent sheer pancake elegance for all occasions.

1 egg, at room temperature
1½ cups milk, at room temperature
3 tablespoons sweet butter, melted, warm
½ teaspoon sugar
½ teaspoon salt
½ cup buckwheat flour
½ cup all-purpose flour, sifted
Vegetable oil
1 cup crème fraîche
1 jar (2 ounces) black or red caviar
Lemon wedges (optional)

Whisk egg until light and foamy. Then gradually whisk in the milk, the melted butter, the sugar, and salt. When thoroughly combined, gradually add buckwheat flour and all-purpose flour to egg mixture, stirring with a whisk just until flours are moistened; do not overmix. Let batter stand, covered, at room temperature for a least 1 hour. Brush a 6-inch crêpe pan or small heavy skillet with a thin film of vegetable oil; heat over medium flame until a few drops of water sizzle several seconds when splashed on pan.

Pour 2 tablespoons of batter into pan; immediately tip pan and rotate to cover bottom evenly with batter. Pour any excess back into bowl. Cook until edges begin to brown and batter is set, about 1 minute.

Turn crêpe, using a flexible spatula; cook until underside is speckled with brown spots, about 30 seconds. Remove crêpe to ovenproof plate; cover loosely with a towel and keep warm in the oven set at lowest heat. Lightly re-oil pan, if necessary; continue to make crêpes until all batter is used, stacking them as they are made on plate in oven.

Serve with the crème fraîche and caviar on the side, and with lemon wedges if desired.

MAKES 16 CRÊPES

CONDIMENTS,
DRESSINGS,
SAUCES

MUSTARD VINAIGRETTE

DILL MUSTARD

CHARLEY'S CHUNKY TOMATO SAUCE

GIL'S BARBECUE SAUCE

MUSTARD VINAIGRETTE

THIS IS A VERY PUNGENT, FULL-FLAVORED DRESSING. THE flavor can be altered by using different oils and vinegars.

3 cloves garlic
½ teaspoon salt
1 teaspoon freshly ground pepper
3 tablespoons Dijon mustard
6 tablespoons balsamic vinegar
½ cup olive oil
½ cup vegetable oil

Mince garlic. With the back of a chopping knife, mash garlic and salt together and place in a 2-cup glass storage jar. Add the pepper, mustard, and vinegar, and blend. Whisk in the olive oil, then the vegetable oil until blended. Let vinaigrette mellow for a least 1 hour.

MAKES 1¼ CUPS

DILL MUSTARD

THIS IS A SWEET AND PUNGENT MUSTARD. IT GOES WELL WITH charcuterie, cold poached shrimp, or gravlax.

½ cup rough whole-grain mustard
½ cup Dijon mustard
1 teaspoon dry mustard powder
3 tablespoons brown sugar
¾–1 cup chopped fresh dill, loosely packed

Combine all ingredients and blend with a fork. Store in a glass jar with a tight lid. Will keep indefinitely in refrigerator.
MAKES 1⅓ CUPS

CHARLEY'S CHUNKY TOMATO SAUCE

A FAST AND SPICY SAUCE TO TOP PASTA, POLENTA, OR seafood.

3 tablespoons extra-virgin olive oil
4 cloves garlic, minced
1 onion, finely chopped
1 can anchovies, drained and coarsely chopped
8 sun-dried tomatoes, coarsely chopped
Pepper to taste (no salt)
1 35-ounce can peeled whole Italian tomatoes, drained and chopped
½ cup chopped parsley
1 tablespoon herbes de Provence (thyme, rosemary, oregano)

Heat oil in a large skillet, and in it briefly sauté the garlic. Add the onions and sauté for 2 minutes. Add the anchovies and sun-dried tomatoes; continue to sauté for another 2 minutes. Add freshly ground pepper (about 8 turns), the tomatoes, parsley, and the herbs. Simmer for 5 minutes.

MAKES ENOUGH SAUCE FOR 4–6 SERVINGS

GIL'S BARBECUE SAUCE

A SWEET AND SPICY SAUCE FOR RIBS OR CHICKEN. SERVE with a Caesar salad, or red and yellow peppers with purple onion in vinaigrette, plus fresh corn and herb butter.

½ pound (2 sticks) butter
1 clove garlic, pressed
1 small onion, chopped
1 teaspoon salt
Freshly ground pepper to taste
1 tablespoon sugar
1½ tablespoons lemon juice
½ cup tomato ketchup
1 tablespoon Worcestershire sauce
½ teaspoon Tabasco sauce

Mix all ingredients together in a large saucepan. Cover, bring to a boil, reduce heat, and simmer for 5 minutes, stirring occasionally.

MAKES ENOUGH SAUCE FOR 4 CHICKEN OR DUCK HALVES, OR 2 RACKS OF RIBS

SOUPS

Lee Bailey's Escarole Soup

Chuck Williams's Leek and Potato Soup

Giorgio DeLuca's Soupe au Pistou

LEE BAILEY'S ESCAROLE SOUP

THE SECRET OF THIS SIMPLE SOUP IS IN THE CHICKEN STOCK. The flavor of the final dish can be no better than the stock you start with. If you use canned stock, enhance its taste by simmering it down a bit (15 minutes or so) with a large onion chopped in it and maybe a stalk of celery. Strain these out before using.

1 medium head escarole, washed
6 cups rich chicken stock, preferably homemade
Salt and pepper to taste
Parmesan cheese

Tear carefully washed escarole leaves into bits, discarding the tough bottom parts. Add this to the stock and simmer for about 15 minutes or until escarole is tender. Correct seasoning with salt and pepper if necessary. Serve with Parmesan cheese on the side.

SERVES 6

CHUCK WILLIAMS'S LEEK AND POTATO SOUP

COOL AND DELICIOUS FOR A WARM SUMMER'S DAY.

4 to 5 medium leeks
1 medium onion
2 tablespoons unsalted butter
4 medium potatoes
4 cups chicken broth, preferably homemade
1 cup milk
1 cup heavy cream
Minced fresh parsley and chopped tomato (or pimiento) for garnish

Trim, wash, and slice leeks (discard tops); peel and slice the onion. Melt butter in a large saucepan, add leeks and onion, and sauté slowly for 10 minutes or until transparent, stirring occasionally. Peel and dice the potatoes, add to leeks together with the broth. Bring to a simmer and cook for another 15 minutes or until potatoes are tender. Scald the milk and add to the vegetables. Bring to a boil, season with salt and pepper, then put through a food mill or purée in a food processor or blender. Chill thoroughly. Before serving swirl in the cream. Garnish with minced parsley and bits of chopped tomato or pimiento.

SERVES 6

GIORGIO DELUCA'S SOUPE AU PISTOU

THIS PROVENÇAL (NIÇOISE) VEGETABLE SOUP IS PERFUMED with a heady pistou of basil and garlic. Bon Appétit!

2 carrots, peeled and chopped
3 leeks, sliced (tender white parts only)
5 medium potatoes, diced
1 pound fresh white beans (or 1 can white navy beans)
Bouquet garni of thyme, parsley, and celery leaves
1 cup elbow macaroni
½ pound green beans, cut into 1-inch lengths
3 zucchini, coarsely chopped
1 tablespoon salt

PISTOU

4 to 5 cloves garlic
1 cup fresh basil leaves, roughly chopped
1 cup freshly grated imported Parmesan cheese
1 cup extra-virgin olive oil (preferably Antinori)
1 fresh tomato, diced
Salt and pepper

Cook all of the vegetables, except the green beans and zucchini, and the bouquet garni in 3 quarts water in a covered casse-

role over medium heat for 30 to 40 minutes. Add the macaroni, green beans, zucchini, and salt, and cook uncovered 15 minutes longer.

Prepare the pistou. Combine the garlic, chopped basil, and cheese in a mortar and pestle. Grind slowly. While grinding slowly drizzle in the olive oil, then add the tomato, salt and pepper. Grind until mixture has formed a rough paste.

When soup is ready stir in 3 to 4 tablespoons of pistou to the pot.

Serve in large soup bowls, with the pistou on the side to be added according to taste. Parmesan may also be sprinkled on top, according to taste.

SERVES 6

VEGETABLES

Asparagus with Lemon Butter

Steaming Broccoli Vinaigrette

String Beans Sesame

Marinated Cucumbers and Onions

Marinated Tomatoes and Onions

Pickled Beets

ASPARAGUS WITH LEMON BUTTER

IN SEASON, ASPARAGUS LOVERS MAKE A WHOLE MEAL OF asparagus, the plainer the better.

2 pounds young asparagus
1 teaspoon salt
2 sticks (16 tablespoons) lightly salted butter
Juice of 1 lemon
3 teaspoons grated lemon peel
8 thick slices of a good white bread

Use a skillet or fish poacher large enough to accommodate the length of the asparagus. Wash asparagus and break off stalks where they snap most easily. Put 2 inches of water in pan, add salt, and bring to a boil. Add asparagus to pan. Return water to a boil, cover, and cook for 2 minutes, or until asparagus are tender but firm. Remove from water and drain asparagus on a clean kitchen towel.

While you are waiting for the water to come to a boil and cooking the asparagus, melt the butter. Add lemon juice and grated lemon, and blend. Toast the bread and place on four warmed plates. Arrange the asparagus on top of the toast and drizzle with lemon butter. Serve at once.

SERVES 4

Note: Vinaigrette is also good on hot or cold asparagus as an appetizer or salad course.

STEAMING BROCCOLI VINAIGRETTE

A SURPRISING TASTE FOR HOT BROCCOLI.

1 large head of broccoli
1 tablespoon salt
⅓ cup vinaigrette

Trim broccoli and cut into bite-size flowerettes. In a large steamer pot (preferably with a colander insert) bring the water to a boil and add the salt. Add the broccoli and return to a boil; let boil for 1 minute and remove broccoli. Quickly shake off excess liquid, then place in a warm bowl and toss with the vinaigrette. Serve hot.

SERVES 4

STRING BEANS SESAME

THESE STRING BEANS HAVE AN ORIENTAL FLAVOR, WHICH WE like to serve with Lemon Chicken, or on a salad plate combined with potatoes vinaigrette and sliced tomatoes.

1 pound young string beans, washed
4 teaspoons sesame seeds, toasted
⅓ cup soy sauce
⅓ cup dry white wine
¼ cup water
1 teaspoon balsamic vinegar
1 clove garlic, pressed
½ teaspoon sugar
¼ teaspoon ground ginger

Toss string beans in a large pot of boiling, heavily salted water. Bring water back to the boil and cook beans for 5 minutes. Pour into a colander and rinse under cold water; drain well. Place string beans in a shallow bowl.

Combine remaining ingredients and pour over string beans. Marinate for at least one hour, tossing occasionally. Serve at room temperature.

SERVES 4–6

MARINATED CUCUMBERS AND ONIONS

THE HEART OF THE SUMMER AND INTO EARLY FALL, WHEN vegetables are plentiful and inexpensive, is the ideal time to prepare marinated or pickled vegetables in large quantities; better still, they are welcome at the table any time of year.

2 cups warm water
1 cup white wine vinegar
¼ cup sugar
1 teaspoon salt
5 large cucumbers
2 medium onions

Combine water, vinegar, sugar, and salt in a glass measuring cup. Peel cucumbers only if the skin is tough. Slice into ¼-inch rounds. Peel and thinly slice onions.

In a glass storage jar, alternate layers of sliced cucumbers and onions. Add brine, and marinate for at least 1 hour before serving.

To store, refrigerate, then allow to return almost to room temperature before serving.

MAKES 2 QUARTS

MARINATED TOMATOES AND ONIONS

U SE A 2-QUART (OR 2-LITER) GLASS STORAGE JAR. NEATLY layer tomatoes and onions, then spoon on "dressing." This makes a delicious lunch, or a "salad" course for dinner. Serve with warm French bread.

8 medium tomatoes, ripe but firm
4 medium onions
1 cup chopped fresh basil (if fresh is not available, omit)
1 teaspoon salt
Freshly ground pepper to taste
2 teaspoons sugar
¼ cup extra-virgin olive oil
½ cup balsamic vinegar

Slice tomatoes into ¼-inch to ½-inch-thick slices. Peel and slice the onions into ¼-inch-thick rings. Layer tomatoes and onion rings in a jar, sprinkling each layer with basil.

In a measuring cup, combine salt, pepper, sugar, olive oil, and vinegar. Mix with a fork and pour over the tomatoes and onions. Marinate at room temperature for at least 1 hour before serving, turning jar several times. Will keep refrigerated for three days; after that the tomatoes get too soggy.

MAKES 2 QUARTS

PICKLED BEETS

A TANGY ADDITION TO ANY GREEN SALAD, ESPECIALLY ONE prepared with fresh arugula. We also like to keep these on hand to add to a French-style crudités course. Serve small portions of julienned carrots, shredded celery root, potatoes vinaigrette, sliced cucumber, and the pickled beets. Add a quartered hard-boiled egg to each plate.

30 medium beets, peeled
1 teaspoon salt
5 tablespoons tarragon vinegar
3 teaspoons sugar

Place the beets in a large saucepan, and add just enough water to cover. Add salt, 3 tablespoons of the tarragon vinegar, and sugar. Bring to a boil and continue cooking for 30 minutes, or until the beets are fork-tender. Do not overcook. Cool for 30 minutes in the liquid.

Remove beets, reserving cooking liquid. Slice or dice beets into bite-size pieces. Spoon the beets into a 2-qt. storage jar.

Combine 1½ cups of the remaining liquid and remaining 2 tablespoons tarragon vinegar. Pour mixture over the beets in the jar. Marinate at room temperature for at least 1 hour, turning the jar several times. The beets will keep refrigerated indefinitely.

MAKES 2 QUARTS

SALADS & SIDE DISHES

PICKLED WEISSWURST

TWICE-COOKED POTATOES
VINAIGRETTE

CORN SALAD IN HUSK

CURLY PASTA SALAD

TED WEIANT'S PICNIC NOODLES WITH SESAME
SAUCE

PICKLED WEISSWURST

W<small>E LIKE TO INCLUDE THIS WITH A CHARCUTERIE ASSORT-</small>
ment for a hearty cocktail party, or at an informal wine tasting.
Serve with a good variety of mustards, a bowl of cornichons,
and crusty breads.

1½ cups water
1 cup white wine
¾ cup tarragon vinegar
2 carrots, scraped and thinly sliced
1 teaspoon mustard seeds
1 teaspoon whole allspice
½ teaspoon whole peppercorns
6 bay leaves
3 cloves garlic, crushed
8 weisswurst

Combine all ingredients, except weisswurst, in an enamel
saucepan, and simmer for 5 minutes. Slice weisswurst into
½-inch rounds, and remove casing. Add weisswurst to poaching
liquid, then remove pan from heat. Cool in poaching liquid to
room temperature.

Transfer to a glass cylinder vase or storage jar for storing and
serving. Serve at room temperature.

S<small>ERVES</small> 8–16

TWICE-COOKED POTATOES VINAIGRETTE

A POTATO LOVER'S DREAM—TANGY POTATO SALAD THE first day, incredible hash browns the next morning for breakfast.

5 pounds very small new potatoes
1 to 2 tablespoons salt
Mustard Vinaigrette (page 28)
Fresh dill, chopped

Wash potatoes and cut in half, but leave the skin on. In a large pot, bring salted water to a boil and add potatoes. Boil just until fork-tender, but not soft. Drain in colander (do not rinse); transfer potatoes to a bowl large enough to hold all 5 pounds.

While potatoes are still hot, drizzle over about half of them a generous amount of mustard vinaigrette. Add the rest of the potatoes, drizzle more vinaigrette over top layer, and sprinkle with dill. Cover and let marinate at room temperature until ready to serve, shaking bowl occasionally to coat all potatoes, adding additional vinaigrette if needed.

FOR A PARTY OF 12–15 PEOPLE

CORN SALAD IN HUSK

IT IS SO PRETTY TO SERVE THIS CORN SALAD IN ITS ORIGINAL container, the husk.

Kernels from 8 ears white or golden corn, 3½–4 cups
4½ cups inexpensive dry champagne or white wine
2 roasted red or green bell peppers, cut into strips, 1 × ⅛ inch
4 sun-dried tomatoes (Pumate San Remo), drained and minced
½ cup olive oil from the sun-dried tomatoes
2 heaping tablespoons minced fresh chives
½ teaspoon salt
Freshly ground pepper to taste

Remove ears from husk carefully, without destroying the husk. Remove silk from inside husk. Prepare salad: Bring 4 cups of

the champagne to a simmer in a medium-size saucepan, add the corn, and cook at a simmer for 5 to 7 minutes, or until the kernels are just tender, still slightly undercooked. Drain, spread the corn out on a plate to cool, and sprinkle with the remaining champagne.

Transfer the corn to a serving bowl, add the remaining ingredients, and combine gently but thoroughly. Stir occasionally, if you are not serving the salad immediately. Place husks on individual plates and scoop salad inside, overflowing a little.

SERVES 8

CURLY PASTA SALAD

WE LOVE PASTA, IN ALL SHAPES AND IN ALL SEASONS. HERE
is a tasty warm-weather salad.

½ box fusilli (½ pound), cooked until tender
2 hard-boiled eggs, chopped
3 stalks celery, diced
½ onion, chopped
4 sun-dried tomatoes, chopped
Mustard Vinaigrette (page 28)
Salt and pepper

Combine fusilli, eggs, celery, onion, and tomatoes. Add enough
vinaigrette to moisten and flavor the salad. Salt and pepper to
taste. This is best when left to marinate for an hour or so, covered, at room temperature.

SERVES 4

TED WEIANT'S PICNIC NOODLES
WITH SESAME SAUCE

A DELIGHTFUL SURPRISE FOR A PICNIC—OR ANY OTHER time. Packed in clear plastic containers, these flavorful noodles are easily transported for dining alfresco.

6 to 8 large cloves garlic

1 cup unsalted chunk-style peanut butter

½ cup soy sauce

½ cup dry white wine or sake

4 teaspoons sesame oil

3 tablespoons hot chili oil

6 tablespoons or about ½ cup minced fresh cilantro, reserve some for
   garnish

6 to 8 tablespoons sugar

1 pound spaghetti (or pasta of your choice)

In a food processor, blender, or bowl chop the garlic—you
should have about 4 tablespoons. Add the peanut butter, soy
sauce, wine, and 3 teaspoons of the sesame oil. Process until
thoroughly blended. Add the chili oil, cilantro, and about 3 to
4 tablespoons of the sugar. Process and blend again. Adjust
sugar to taste. Allow sauce to "ripen" for several hours or
overnight. Sauce keeps indefinitely and improves with age.

Cook spaghetti until barely tender and still a bit firm. Drain in
a colander and rinse under cold water; drain well. Spread out
on a clean kitchen towel and pat dry. Put in a large bowl and
toss gently with remaining 1 teaspoon sesame oil. Chill. Before
serving, toss again with a little sesame oil, if desired, and
cilantro.

For taking on a picnic, you could combine the sauce and noodles at home, or package them separately, and let guests help
themselves.

MAKES ENOUGH FOR ABOUT 6 PEOPLE

ONE-DISH MEALS & SIMPLE ENTRÉES

Charley's Chili

Gold Cornbread Fillets

Grilled Japanese Shrimp

Charley's Drunken Shrimp

Grilled Fresh Tuna

Spinach Capellini

Richard Giglio's Risotto

Omelette in a Bread Box

Felipe Rojas-Lombardi's Roast Pepper,
Basil, and Cheese Pie

Veal and Ham Loaf

Lemon Chicken

CHARLEY'S CHILI

TOPPED WITH A CORNBREAD CRUST, HERE IS A NEW WAY TO spruce up an old favorite, which we make in simple ovenproof restaurant-ware bowls. It's an especially sturdy dish for a hungry group.

6 cups of your favorite chili recipe, heated
1 cup yellow cornmeal
1 cup all-purpose flour
¼ cup sugar
4 teaspoons baking powder
½ teaspoon salt
1 cup milk
1 egg
¼ cup melted butter
Sour cream for garnish

Heat oven to 425°. Put 1 cup of heated chili in each bowl, or fill to within 1 inch from top of bowl.

Combine the cornmeal, flour, sugar, baking powder, and salt in a mixing bowl. Add the milk, egg, and butter. Beat with a fork until smooth, about 1 minute.

Place bowls filled with chili on a cookie sheet. Pour batter over hot chili just to cover. Bake for about 25 minutes, or until crust is golden brown. Serve steaming hot, with a dollop of sour cream atop each bowl, and a bowl of sour cream on the side.

SERVES 6

GOLD CORNBREAD FILLETS

Even non-fish eaters and kids like these crunchy, easy fish fillets. Spice and dress up with Charley's Chunky Tomato Sauce (page 30).

3 large lemon sole fillets
¾ cup balsamic vinegar
1 cup yellow cornmeal
½ cup flour
½ teaspoon salt
1 teaspoon pepper
4 tablespoons butter, melted
1 lemon, thinly sliced for garnish

Preheat oven to 450°. Cut fillets into 2-inch strips across the width. Place in a shallow bowl and marinate in balsamic vinegar for about 10 minutes.

Combine dry ingredients on a platter. Shake excess vinegar off fillets and coat each strip with flour mixture. Place strips on an ungreased jellyroll pan, and drizzle over them melted butter. Bake for 20 minutes, or until golden. Garnish with thin lemon slices, and serve. (These may be eaten hot or cold.)

Serves 6

GRILLED JAPANESE SHRIMP

SHRIMP WITH A TANGY, SLIGHTLY JAPANESE FLAVOR.

3 to 4 large shrimp per person (depending on size)
Tuna marinade plus 3 heaping tablespoons brown sugar and juice of 1
  orange (page 68)

Peel and devein shrimp, leaving tails on. Prepare the marinade.
Marinate shrimp in a shallow glass platter for 1 hour, covered,
in the refrigerator. Grill on a hibachi, outdoor grill, or under
the broiler about 5 minutes per side, depending on size.
Serve at once, using remaining marinade as dip at the table.
MAKES ENOUGH MARINADE FOR UP TO 6 SERVINGS OF SHRIMP

CHARLEY'S DRUNKEN SHRIMP

AN ELEGANT FIRST COURSE.

16 large shrimp
2 cloves garlic, minced
½ cup olive oil
1 large onion, peeled and sliced
Salt and pepper to taste
Juice of ½ lemon
1 lemon, seeded and thinly sliced
½ cup dry white wine

Peel and devein shrimp, leaving the tails on. In a large skillet sauté the garlic in the olive oil for 2 minutes. Add the sliced onion and salt and pepper. Sauté until the onions become transparent. Add shrimp and sauté for 2 minutes, or until the shrimp turn pink. Add lemon juice, the lemon slices, and white wine, and cook for another 2 minutes.

Remove from skillet and let cool to room temperature. Arrange shrimp artfully on a serving platter or on individual plates.

SERVES 4

Note: The shrimp may be refrigerated overnight. Bring back to room temperature before serving.

Grilled Fresh Tuna

For fish and meat lovers alike, tuna steak is a favorite.

1¼-inch tuna steaks (½ pound per person)

Marinade

2 tablespoons finely minced fresh ginger
2 teaspoons finely minced fresh garlic
2 teaspoons lemon zest
¼ cup soy sauce
¾ cup white wine

Combine all ingredients in a shallow glass or china platter. Marinate tuna for 1 hour, turning several times (do not refrigerate).

Grill on a hibachi, outdoor grill, or under the broiler for 3 to 4 minutes per side, basting with marinade. Do not overcook, for a slightly undercooked center is best with fresh tuna.

Makes enough marinade for up to 6 tuna steaks

SPINACH CAPELLINI

THE SURPRISE IN THIS DISH IS THE ZESTY FLAVOR OF FRESH lemon slices.

4 tablespoons butter
3 tablespoons olive oil
6 cloves garlic, sliced about ⅛-inch thick
3 pounds fresh spinach, washed, patted dry, stems removed
¾ teaspoon salt
Coarsely ground pepper to taste
1 thinly sliced lemon, seeded
Juice from ½ lemon
½ cup chicken broth
1 pound capellini #9 (use dried pasta)
Freshly grated Parmesan cheese

Use a large heavy skillet, and heat the butter and olive oil until bubbly. Add the garlic and sauté on medium-low heat until nut brown, but be careful not to burn. Add the spinach, salt, and pepper and toss, using large tongs. Sauté until spinach is slightly wilted, about 3 to 4 minutes. Add sliced lemon and toss, cooking another 3 to 4 minutes. Combine lemon juice and chicken broth and add to the spinach.

In 4 to 6 quarts of boiling salted water, cook the capellini until just tender, about 3 minutes from boiling point. Drain, and divide among individual bowls. Spoon spinach-and-lemon broth over capellini.

Serve with a bowl of freshly grated Parmesan cheese.

SERVES 4 AS A MAIN COURSE

RICHARD GIGLIO'S RISOTTO

SERVE THIS RISOTTO WITH SOFT-BOILED EGGS WHICH HAVE almost cooled, a platter of sliced garden tomatoes, and slices of thick country bread, toasted after having been spread with olive oil. Pass a bowl of freshly grated Romano cheese.

8 tablespoons butter
1 onion, chopped
2 cups Italian Arborio rice
5 cups homemade chicken broth, or canned
1 cup grated Parmesan or Romano cheese (use ½ for serving at the table)

Sauté chopped onion in 4 tablespoons of the butter in a heavy saucepan until transparent, but not brown. Add the rice and continue to sauté until rice takes on a bit of color, about 4 minutes.

Heat broth to a boil in a separate saucepan; then keep at a simmer. Begin adding broth a little bit at a time (about ½ cup), and stir until the broth is absorbed.

When the rice is cooked, but still al dente, remove from heat. Stir in the remaining 4 tablespoons of butter, plus ½ cup of the cheese.

Transfer to a large heated platter. Serve hot.

SERVES 4

Omelette in a Bread Box

For a cool-weather picnic, take along a hearty omelette, kept warm inside its own "bread box."

1 large round French bread (10 to 12 inches in diameter)
2 tablespoons olive oil
2 tablespoons butter
4 medium new potatoes, washed, dried, and thinly sliced
1 medium onion, diced
2 cloves garlic, mashed and chopped
2 medium zucchini, thinly sliced
¾ teaspoon salt
Freshly ground pepper
9 eggs, beaten well
3 rounded tablespoons Parmesan cheese

Heat oven to 350°. Cut bread in half horizontally. Partially hollow out center of each half, leaving about 1 inch of soft bread and crust. Melt the oil and butter in a 10-inch omelette pan. Brush about 1 tablespoon of the oil and butter inside bread halves. Reassemble loaf and wrap in heavy foil. Place in oven while preparing omelette.

Add potatoes, onion, and garlic to the pan, turning often, about 4 to 5 minutes, over medium heat. Add zucchini and sauté for about 3 minutes. The potatoes should be nicely browned and the zucchini translucent.

Add salt and pepper to beaten eggs and pour over vegetables. Cook omelette over low heat, pushing edge of the omelette toward the center so that the runny eggs run off and begin to set. Cook until the top is just set, but still moist. Run a spatula around the edge, adding a little butter to loosen the omelette from the pan. Sprinkle grated Parmesan cheese over top of the omelette. Then, place the pan in the oven and heat for 6 minutes to set the eggs. Remove the bread from the oven, open and slide omelette into bottom half of bread, then quickly replace top to form a box. Wrap in several layers of heavy foil to keep toasty warm for hours.

SERVES 6

FELIPE ROJAS-LOMBARDI'S ROAST PEPPER, BASIL, AND CHEESE PIE

PASTRY CRUST—ONE 8-INCH SHELL

1½ cups all-purpose flour

¾ teaspoon salt

6 tablespoons sweet butter, chilled

2 tablespoons Crisco or vegetable shortening

1 to 2 tablespoons ice water

ROASTED PEPPERS

4 red peppers (1½ pounds)

3 tablespoons olive oil or vegetable oil

CUSTARD

4 eggs

2 egg yolks

2 cups heavy cream

2 ounces goat cheese

2 ounces grated Gruyère, Emmenthaler, or Jarlsberg

1 teaspoon salt or to taste

8 tablespoons thinly sliced scallions (white part only)

¼ cup tightly packed basil leaves, thinly shredded

½ teaspoon fresh hot chili pepper (seeded and finely chopped) or ½ teaspoon dry chili pepper

8 to 12 perfectly uniform fresh basil leaves for garnish

Prepare the dough. Place the flour and salt in a bowl. Working quickly, slice the chilled butter thinly and add to the bowl along with the shortening. Using fingertips, swiftly incorporate flour with butter and shortening until mixture forms a mealy or crumbly texture. Sprinkle with ice water a little at a time and knead mixture into a smooth ball. Place in plastic wrap and refrigerate for a half hour.

Remove dough from refrigerator and place on a lightly floured work surface. Using a rolling pin, flatten the ball of dough into a 1-inch-thick, 6-inch-round slab; proceed to roll it out to an even $\frac{1}{8}$-inch-thick circle. Gently fold the circle in half and in half again to form a quarter circle. Place into an $8\frac{1}{2}$-inch pie tin and open the folded dough carefully and evenly, allowing a 2-inch measure of dough to hang down from the edge of the pie tin. Using your fingertips, lightly press the dough to the bottom and edges of the pie tin. Gently roll the hanging dough upwards toward the edge of the pie tin, and with a fork, press down to form a neat design around the pastry shell. Prick the bottom of the shell with a fork and line with a sheet of foil or parchment paper.

Fill this liner with plenty of dried beans and bake in a preheated 400° oven for 15 minutes. Then turn heat down to 350° and bake an additional 15 minutes. Remove beans and liner and continue to bake for 15 to 20 minutes or until crust is lightly golden. Cool on a rack.

Rub the peppers thoroughly with the oil. Place on a rack and into a preheated 500° oven for approximately $\frac{1}{2}$ hour, turning to roast peppers evenly. When peppers are done—they will collapse —remove from oven. When cool enough to handle, cut each pepper in half with a paring knife. Using a teaspoon, remove seeds and gently pull away the stem and skin with your fingers or a paring knife if necessary. Be careful to leave the flesh intact. Sprinkle very lightly with a pinch of salt and roll each half-pepper. You should end up with 8 rolls about 4 inches long. Set aside.

Finally, make the custard. In a bowl, beat the eggs and egg yolks, then add the heavy cream. Crumble in the goat cheese and add along with the grated Gruyère, salt, scallions, shredded basil, and hot pepper. Mix thoroughly. Gently pour mixture into pre-baked pastry shell and garnish the surface with a spiral design of roasted red pepper rolls. Place into a preheated 350° oven for about 45 minutes or until set.

Remove from oven when done, and immediately place the whole basil leaves between the red pepper rolls in an alternating pattern. Brush surface lightly with olive oil and allow to cool for 10 to 15 minutes before serving.

SERVES 6

Veal and Ham Loaf

Served at room temperature and thinly sliced, this loaf is a light meat course, ideal for a warm-weather meal.

2 pounds ground veal
1 pound ground ham
2 teaspoons salt
½ teaspoon freshly ground pepper
½ teaspoon dried thyme (if fresh thyme, use more)
2 eggs, lightly beaten
2 tablespoons Cognac
1½ cups seasoned bread crumbs
Fresh rosemary or other herbs for garnish

Preheat oven to 350°. In large bowl, mix all ingredients together. Grease a large roasting pan. With your hands, shape a loaf as long as the pan, but only about 5 inches wide to create a long narrow loaf (like a fillet of beef). Bake 2 hours.

Cool in pan. Loosen bottom with spatula, and remove carefully. Slice about ⅜-inch thick. Arrange sliced loaf on a fish platter (or other long platter). Garnish with fresh rosemary or other herbs or leaves.

Serves 10

LEMON CHICKEN

W_E LIKE THE ZING OF LEMON IN SO MANY FOODS ... IT ADDS just enough snap to these chicken breasts.

3 whole chicken breasts, split, skinned, and boned
1 teaspoon salt
½ tablespoon fresh ground pepper
1 cup flour
3 to 4 tablespoons butter
2 cloves garlic, sliced
Juice of 1 fresh lemon
1 whole lemon, thinly sliced

Wash and pat dry chicken breasts. Blend salt, pepper, and flour in a shallow bowl, and lightly dredge chicken.

Over a medium flame, heat the butter in a skillet. Sauté the sliced garlic until it is golden, then discard. Add the chicken breasts to the skillet and sauté for 6 to 8 minutes on each side, until golden brown. Add the lemon juice and continue cooking for 1 minute. Remove chicken and put on warm serving platter, or individual plates. Garnish with two thin slices of lemon on each chicken breast. This also makes a good cold entrée.

SERVES 6

DESSERTS

ALMOND CRUNCH

ZESTY BOSC PEARS

SECKEL PEARS ALMONDINE

ORANGES IN PORT WINE

CRANBERRY/MAPLE APPLES

PEARS WITH STILTON CORES

THE SILVER PALATE'S LIME MOUSSE

THE SILVER PALATE'S GRAND MARNIER
CHOCOLATE MOUSSE

4TH OF JULY CAKE

PERI'S LEMON SQUARES

CHOCOLATE BROWNIES IN DOILIES

MISS REMY'S MADELEINES

ELI ZABAR'S SHORTBREAD COOKIES

ALMOND CRUNCH

A CRUNCHY CANDYLIKE TOPPING FOR ICE CREAM THAT IS quick and easy, yet elegant when served in stemmed goblets.

2 tablespoons butter
1 cup slivered almonds
¼ cup brown sugar

In a heavy skillet, melt butter until bubbly. Add the almonds and sauté until toasty brown. Add brown sugar and continue to cook until sugar is melted (about 2 minutes). Spoon hot over coffee or vanilla ice cream. Serve at once.

SERVES 6

ZESTY BOSC PEARS

P OACHED FRUIT IS DELICIOUS, AND ONCE MADE, THERE IS always a ready supply on hand. This recipe for Bosc pears serves as the master instruction for the other poached pear, orange, and apple desserts that follow.

6 whole, firm Bosc pears
2 cups sweet sherry
1 cup light corn syrup
1 piece star anise, available in Oriental food stores (optional)

1 1½-inch piece vanilla bean
¼ cup each of lemon, orange, and lime peel strips
Fresh mint leaves for garnish

Wash and peel pears. Leave stems intact. In a stainless steel, enamelware, or glass pot large enough to hold a single layer of fruit, combine sherry, corn syrup, anise, vanilla bean, and citrus peel. Bring to a boil. Add fruit. Simmer, uncovered, until just softened but not mushy, or about ten to fifteen minutes. Do not overcook. Remove from heat and let cool. Store, covered in poaching liquid, in tightly covered container in refrigerator until ready to serve. Keeps for several weeks. To serve, transfer fruit to decorative glass serving dish and spoon on liquid. Garnish with mint leaves. SERVES 6

SECKEL PEARS ALMONDINE

1 cup light corn syrup
1 cup water
1 cup Amaretto liqueur
1½ pieces crystallized ginger, thinly sliced
About 12 Seckel pears (a tiny variety), scrubbed and unpeeled
¼ cup sliced almonds for garnish

Combine corn syrup, water, liqueur, and ginger, and bring to a boil. Continue with poaching instructions for Bosc pear recipe. To serve, garnish with almonds. SERVES 6

ORANGES IN PORT WINE

3 cups tawny port
1 cinnamon stick
½ teaspoon juniper berries
½ teaspoon whole cloves
6 peeled navel oranges

Combine port and spices and bring to a boil. Add fruit and continue with poaching instructions for the Bosc pear recipe.
SERVES 6

CRANBERRY/MAPLE APPLES

1 12-ounce bottle maple-flavored syrup
1 cup light corn syrup
¼ cup cranberry-flavored liqueur or juice
½ teaspoon whole allspice
6 firm, tart, peeled cooking apples, stems intact

Combine syrups, cranberry liqueur, and allspice, and bring to a boil. Continue with poaching instructions for the Bosc pear recipe.
SERVES 6

Pears with Stilton Cores

CHEESE AND FRUIT ALL IN ONE, AND VERY PRETTY. BE CERtain to buy firm, beautiful pears with stems, preferably a little underripe.

6 Bosc pears (1 per person)
Juice of ½ lemon
½ pound Stilton cheese, at room temperature

With apple corer, core pears working from the bottom almost up to the stem. Stop coring about ½ inch from stem and twist core free. Remove core and immediately sprinkle inside of pears with lemon juice.

Cut a wedge of cheese a little larger than core, and then, using your fingers, push the cheese firmly into the pears. Wrap in plastic wrap and refrigerate until the cheese is firm, about 1½ hours.

When ready to serve, slice each pear crosswise into ¼-inch circles, then reassemble on individual plates.

SERVES 6

THE SILVER PALATE'S LIME MOUSSE

Tart and buttery lime mousse has been one of the Silver Palate's most popular desserts for years.

8 tablespoons (1 stick) sweet butter
5 eggs
1 cup granulated sugar
¾ cup fresh lime juice (6 or 7 limes)
Grated zest of 5 limes
2 cups heavy cream, chilled

Melt the butter in the top of a double boiler over simmering water. Beat eggs and sugar in a bowl until light and foamy. Slowly add mixture to melted butter, stirring constantly. Cook gently until mixture becomes a custard, about 10 minutes (do not overcook or eggs will scramble). Remove custard from heat and stir in the lime juice and grated zest. Cool to room temperature.

This step is unorthodox but crucial. Using an electric mixer, whip chilled cream until very stiff—almost, but not quite, to the point where it would become butter. Fold lime custard into whipped cream until just blended. Pour into 8 individual pots de crème, wineglasses, or goblets.

SERVES 8

THE SILVER PALATE'S GRAND MARNIER
CHOCOLATE MOUSSE

A FABULOUS EXPERIENCE FOR ANYONE WHO ADORES
chocolate.

1½ pounds semisweet chocolate chips
½ cup prepared espresso coffee
½ cup Grand Marnier
4 egg yolks
2 cups heavy cream, chilled
¼ cup granulated sugar
8 egg whites
Pinch of salt
½ teaspoon vanilla extract
Candied rosebuds for garnish (optional)

Melt chocolate chips in a heavy saucepan over very low heat,
stirring; add the espresso, then stir in the Grand Marnier. Let
cool to room temperature. Add egg yolks, one at a time, beating thoroughly after each addition.

Whip 1 cup of the cream until thickened, then gradually add
in the sugar, beating until stiff. Beat egg whites with salt until
stiff. Gently fold egg whites into whipped cream.

Stir about one third of cream and egg white mixture thoroughly into the chocolate. Then scrape remaining cream and egg mixture over lightened chocolate base and fold gently. Pour into 8 individual dessert cups or a serving bowl. Refrigerate for 2 hours, or until set.

At serving time, whip remaining cup of cream until thickened, add vanilla and whip to form soft peaks. Top each portion of the mousse with a share of the cream and the candied rosebuds, if desired.

SERVES 8

4TH OF JULY CAKE

Most people have a favorite white or yellow cake recipe, so use yours for this 4th of July cake. The art of this dessert lies in the decorating and the berries.

Double recipe for layer cake
2 pints heavy cream
1 tablespoon confectioners' sugar
1 teaspoon vanilla extract
2 pints strawberries
1 pint blueberries

Preheat oven to 350°. Grease and flour a 17-by-12-by-½-inch roasting pan. Make up your cake recipe and pour into pan. So that you get a flat top cake, spread batter a little higher on sides and lower in the middle. Bake for 50 minutes. Test center for doneness with a toothpick. If it comes out clean, remove cake from oven. If center is still moist, bake 5 minutes longer and test again. When cake is done, run a knife around the edges and let cake cool. Whip cream just until it starts to thicken. Add the confectioners' sugar and vanilla. Continue beating until the cream forms soft peaks. When cake is cool, pour all of the whipped cream on top and spread so that the cream covers the top of the cake. Rinse, core, and slice strawberries in half ver-

tically, then blot on paper towel. Rinse blueberries and pour onto paper towel to dry. With a knife, mark a rectangle in the upper left corner 6 inches long by 5½ inches wide and fill with blueberries. To form stripes with the sliced strawberries, start at the top of the cake next to the blueberries. Make 2 rows very close to each other. Then across the bottom of the cake make another 2 rows of strawberries. Do a third double row in the center of the cake, starting under the blueberries. For a touch of whimsy, place one whole strawberry with a stem at the end of the final row.

SERVES 24

PERI'S LEMON SQUARES

THIS IS OUR FAVORITE SWEET TO SERVE WITH A FRESH FRUIT dessert.

½ cup butter (1 stick), at room temperature
1 cup all-purpose flour
¼ cup confectioners' sugar
A pinch of salt

LEMON TOPPING

2 eggs
1 cup granulated sugar
¼ teaspoon salt
Juice and zest of 1 lemon
¼ cup flour
½ teaspoon baking powder
Confectioners' sugar

Preheat oven to 350°. In a food processor cream together the first four ingredients, until they form a ball. With your fingers press the dough onto the bottom of a lightly buttered 8-inch baking pan. Bake for 20 minutes.

While the square is baking, prepare the lemon topping. Beat

eggs well, gradually adding the sugar. While continuing to beat the eggs and sugar, slowly add the remaining ingredients. Reduce oven to 325°. Pour the topping over the hot, baked shortbread, and return to the oven at once. Bake for 30 to 35 minutes, until the top is light gold. Remove the pan and run a sharp knife around the edges of the square. Cool for about 20 minutes, cut into squares, remove from pan, and arrange on a pretty serving plate or cake stand.

Sprinkle with confectioners' sugar.

MAKES 9 SQUARES

CHOCOLATE BROWNIES IN DOILIES

THE PRETTY LACY EDGE OF PAPER DOILIES MAKES THESE gooey brownies real party fare.

2 sticks (1 cup) lightly salted butter
3 squares bitter chocolate
2 cups sugar
4 eggs, beaten
Pinch of salt
2 teaspoons vanilla extract
1⅔ cups flour
6-inch paper doilies
Confectioners' sugar

Preheat oven to 350°. In top of double boiler, melt butter and chocolate. Cool slightly. Whisk in sugar, then eggs, salt, and vanilla. Mix well. Stir in flour.

With fingertips, press each paper doily into the well of an ungreased muffin tin. Using a ladle, fill halfway with brownie mixture, doing one at a time (the weight of the mixture will hold the doily "cup" in place). Be careful not to drip mixture on the lacy edge of doily. Bake at 350° for about 30 minutes on center rack, until done. Cool.

Sprinkle with confectioners' sugar.

MAKES 16–18 BROWNIES

Miss Remy's Madeleines

THE "EXTRAORDINARY THING" THAT HAPPENED TO PROUST
happens to everyone who tastes these fabulous madeleines. We
had a fantastic response to Miss Remy's madeleines at Wolfman •
Gold & Good Company. If you can keep from eating them your-
self, they make a wonderful gift.

4 whole eggs, extra large
1 egg yolk
1½ cups fine sugar
1 teaspoon vanilla extract
2 cups flour, sifted
1½ teaspoons lemon zest
1 teaspoon orange zest
1½ cups clarified butter
Confectioners' sugar

Preheat oven to 375°. Using a small pastry brush, grease
madeleine molds. Combine eggs, egg yolk, sugar, and vanilla in
a large bowl, and heat over hot water. When the eggs are warm,
remove from heat and beat in a mixer at high speed for about
15 minutes until the eggs are light and fluffy. They should triple
in bulk. Fold the flour and lemon and orange zest into the eggs,
then fold in the clarified butter. Spoon rounded tablespoons of

the batter into the greased molds. Bake for 7 to 10 minutes, or until the tops are golden brown. Let the madeleines cool, then sprinkle lightly with confectioners' sugar.

MAKES 4 DOZEN MADELEINES

Note: Tightly covered, the madeleines will keep for up to two weeks. The longer they sit, the better they are with tea or coffee.

Eli Zabar's Shortbread Cookies

THESE SHORTBREAD COOKIES ARE EVEN MORE OF A TREAT when cut into heart shapes.

¾ cup butter, at room temperature
½ cup sugar
½ teaspoon vanilla extract
1¾ cups flour
Pinch of salt

Preheat oven to 350°. Cream the butter and sugar until well mixed, then blend in the vanilla extract. Add some salt to the flour, then combine flour and butter mixture. Refrigerate, after mixing, for 30 minutes.

Roll out chilled dough to ½-inch-thick sheet. Cut heart-shaped sections from the dough, and place them on silicone baking paper on a cookie sheet. Bake for about 20 minutes, or until cookies are light brown.

MAKES APPROXIMATELY 24 COOKIES

DRINKS

BELLINI

MIMOSA

WHITE WINE SANGRIA

BELLINI

THIS IS A CLASSIC AT HARRY'S BAR IN VENICE. IT IS A WONDER-ful brunch drink or summer aperitif.

4 ripe peaches
1 bottle of champagne

Peel and slice the ripe peaches into the bowl of a food processor. Blend for about 1 minute.

Place a generous tablespoon of peach purée in the bottom of an oversized balloon wineglass. When ready to serve, pop the cork on a chilled bottle of your favorite champagne and fill the glasses halfway. Give one stir to combine. Saluti!

SERVES 6

White Wine Sangria

A LIGHTER VERSION OF THE TRADITIONAL RED SANGRIA.

1 bottle of dry white wine
Juice of 2 oranges
1 orange, thinly sliced
1 lime, thinly sliced
1 lemon, thinly sliced
1 peach, peeled and sliced
¼ cup extra-fine sugar
Club soda

Combine all ingredients except the club soda in a large glass pitcher. Stir. Refrigerate until ready to serve. When ready to serve, fill large wineglasses halfway, spooning several pieces of fruit into each. Add ice and top with club soda.

SERVES 6

MIMOSA

NOTHING COULD BE SIMPLER OR MORE STYLISH THAN A mimosa at a Sunday brunch. To make an excellent one only requires the best ingredients.

1 quart freshly squeezed orange juice
1 orange, sliced
1 bottle of your favorite champagne

Use large balloon or tulip wineglasses. Fill about ⅓ full with orange juice. Place a slice of orange on the rim of each glass. When ready to serve, top off with champagne.

SERVES 6